Jerusalem in Needlepoint and Embroidery

by ann roth

EIGHTEEN MEMORABLE SITES OF JERUSALEM IN FULL COLOR

FOR CROSS-STITCHING WITH DESCRIPTIONS AND DETAILED INSTRUCTIONS

Foreword by RUTH DAYAN

W. FOULSHAM & Co. Ltd., Yeovil Road, Slough, Bucks.

Layout by Gaby de Vries-Shay

First British Edition published by W. Foulsham & Co. Ltd., 1973

Produced by Massada Press Ltd., Jerusalem

© 1972 by Massada Press Ltd., Jerusalem

Library of Congress Catalog Card No. 72-3129
ISBN 0-572-00848-1

Printed in Israel
by Peli Printing Works Ltd., Givatayim

Jerusalem has been depicted pictorially innumerable times and in almost every form imaginable. It now gives me great pleasure to introduce Jerusalem in an embroidered form.

The embroidered sites in this book should be considered a direct continuation of the handicraft tradition from Biblical times. It is with pride that I recommend this book to the women of the world.

Israel's handicrafts are in the process of unequalled development due to the influence of world cultures in the area where all religions meet. I feel fortunate in being connected with this cultural development and being able to encourage an interest and deep love for Jerusalem through fine embroidery.

RUTH DAYAN
President
MASKIT Israel Center of Handicrafts

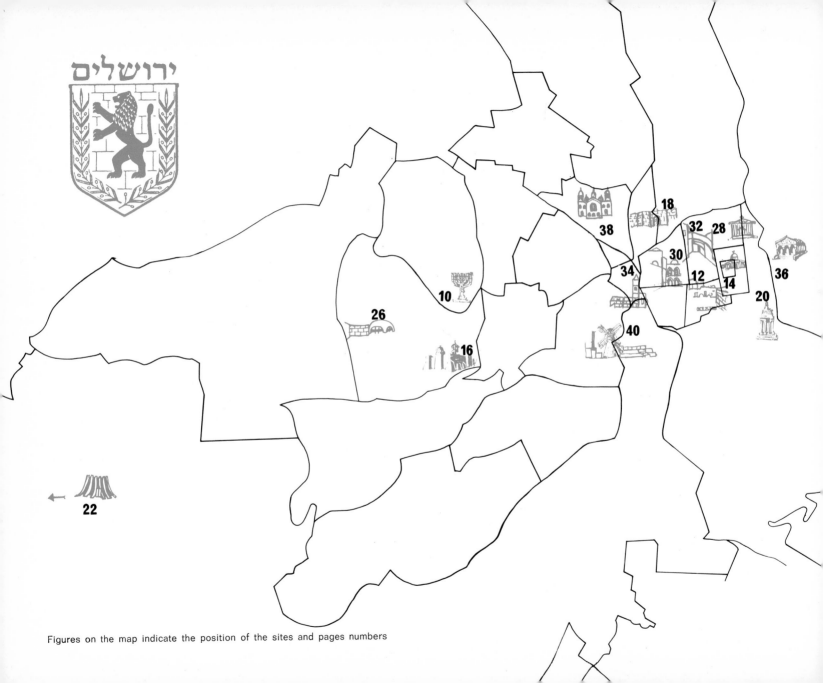

ירושלים

10

26

16

22

38

18

32 28

30

34

12

14

40

20

36

Figures on the map indicate the position of the sites and pages numbers

CONTENTS

ירושלים

ABOUT JERUSALEM

Jerusalem means 'city of peace,' yet in its 4,000 years of tumultuous history it has been fought over more than any other place on earth. Intimately linked with mankind's highest aspirations throughout the ages, its rocky foundations are venerated by a billion people scattered over the globe.

It was here that Abraham took his only son Isaac for sacrifice, the very same place that a red-haired shepherd king called David captured from the Jebusites. This was the city of Solomon's Temple, the city of Babylonian destruction, the city of Ezra and Nehemia. Here Herod the tyrant king built the Temple and resplendent public buildings for his unloving subjects. The Passion and Crucifixion of Jesus made this city holy to Christians and it is venerated by Moslems because of the vision of Mohammed in which he ascended to heaven from Mt. Moriah: Jerusalem of David's star, Jerusalem of the crescent, Jerusalem of the cross.

Babylonians, Romans, Byzantines, Persians, Crusaders, Mamelukes, are only a few of the nations that have conquered the city. They have come and gone, swallowed up in time. Jerusalem remains eternal, a mystical city of prophesy, of prayer, of life.

In 1967, after 19 years of strife and division, Jerusalem was re-united by the same nation that had made it great. Today it is a dynamic and exciting city, all its holy places accessible to pilgrims, once more aspiring to be Jerusalem — City of Peace.

מפת מידבא

THE MADEBA MAP

This ancient view of the walled city of Jerusalem comes from the 'Madeba Map,' the oldest known representation of the Holy Land, which dates from the sixth century C.E. It formed part of the mosaic pavement that covered the floor before the altar of the Byzantine church of Madeba in Transjordan.

The artists and craftsmen who made the map, so long ago, formed the tiny stones of the mosaic into an impressionistic picture of the Holy Land, showing the sites connected with the life of Jesus, for instance the River Jordan and the place where His baptism was believed to have taken place.

As to Jerusalem, the map presents a bird's eye view of the city, on a scale much bigger than that applied to other features. The walls and gates, the main streets, churches and public buildings are clearly distinguishable.

Originally, the map was 24 meters wide by six deep. It represented not only the Holy Land, but also those parts of the neighboring countries connected with Biblical history: Lower Egypt, the Sinai Peninsula and the southern part of Syria.

Unfortunately, a great part of the enormous original mosaic had already been destroyed when the map was discovered in 1884, and further damage was caused during the construction of the new church. Even so, what remains offers the modern historian invaluable visual testimony on 6th century Jerusalem and the traditional holy sites.

A mosaic reproduction of the section of the map showing the view of Jerusalem decorates the floor of the entrance-hall of the elegant Y.M.C.A. building in West Jerusalem.

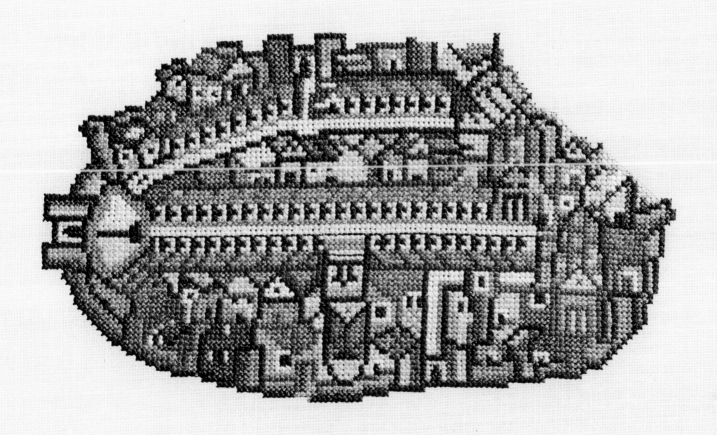

ירושלים

THE KNESSET MENORAH

'And the Lord spake unto Moses saying . . . and thou shalt make a candlestick of pure gold . . . and there be six branches going out of the side thereof, three branches of the candlestick out of the one side thereof and three branches of the candlestick out of the other side thereof . . . and thou shalt make the lamps thereof seven.' (Exodus 25, 31–37) The seven-branched golden candlestick, the Menorah, made in accordance with the Divine commandment, was lighted every day, first in the Tent of Meeting in the desert, and later on in the Temple of Jerusalem until the day of its destruction by the Romans (70 C.E.). The victors carried the Menorah to Rome with the rest of their booty, and it served as a showpiece in the triumph of Titus. Its appearance is preserved in all its splendor in the relief decorating the Arch of Titus in Rome.

Representations of the Menorah, in relief, in painting or in mosaic, decorated every synagogue in the Holy Land and abroad, in the Talmudic period and later on. They are also to be found on sarcophagi, on tombstones and on lintels over the doors of Jewish homes. The Menorah had become a symbol of the spiritual values of Judaism. No wonder that the State of Israel chose the Menorah as its official symbol.

Opposite the modernistic wrought-iron gate to the Knesset, the Israeli Parliament, stands a big bronze Menorah, a gift of the British Parliament to Israel's House of Representatives. This Menorah is a work of the Jewish sculptor Benno Elkan, an artist who has revived the medieval art of making decorated bronze chandeliers. His chandeliers are to be found in Westminster Abbey and other churches in England. But his masterpiece is the Knesset Menorah decorated with scenes from Biblical history.

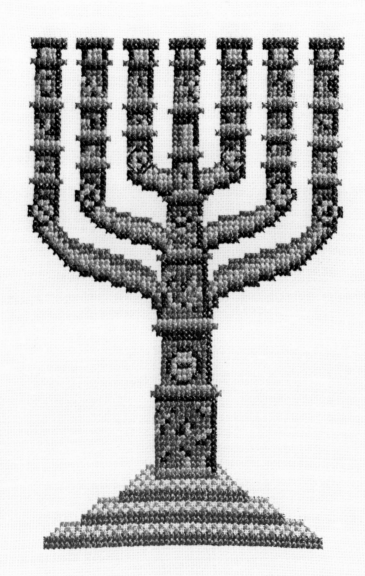

הכותל המערבי

THE WESTERN WALL

When the legions of Titus conquered Jerusalem, in the year 70 C.E., they systematically destroyed the town, leaving intact, besides three towers of Herod's palace, only the Western Wall of the Temple enclosure. The Roman 10th legion, which garrisoned the city, set up its camp nearby.

The Western Wall formed part of the retaining walls supporting the vast platform constructed around the summit of Mount Moriah, on which the now destroyed Temple had stood. For the Jews, this wall was the sole surviving remnant of their Sanctuary, the sorrowful memento of their lost national independence. Hither they came to wail and to pray, particularly on the Ninth of Av, the fast-day commemorating the destruction of the Temple. When, by edict of the Emperor Hadrian, they were forbidden access to the rebuilt city, they used to bribe the guards, thus 'buying the privilege of shedding their tears on the ruins of their town,' as the Church Father Jerome recounts.

Thus, throughout the centuries, the Western Wall was known as the Wailing Wall and was holy to the Jewish people. Pious pilgrims from everywhere in the Diaspora came to kiss the stones of this wall, from which, according to Jewish tradition, the Divine Presence has never departed.

Often it was a dangerous undertaking and, during the nineteen years of Arab occupation of the Old City, from 1948 to 1967, Jews were denied access to this holy place altogether. When the Israeli Defense Army entered the Old City in 1967, the soldiers rushed, first of all, to the Western Wall. No longer a Wailing Wall, it has now become a symbol of recovered national independence. It is today a place of continuous fervent prayer, and often also a place of spontaneous joy, finding its expression in song and dance.

THE DOME OF THE ROCK

Its shining golden dome the dominant feature of the Old City's skyline, the Dome of the Rock is Jerusalem's loveliest building, the third most holy Moslem site and one of the most beautiful mosques in the world.

It stands within the vast square built to enclose the summit of Mount Moriah on which the Temple stood until its destruction by the Romans. Jews still call it 'the Square of Temple Mount,' while for Moslems this is 'al Haram esh Sharif,' the Noble Sanctuary.

The mosque is still popularly known as 'the Mosque of Omar,' although this is misleading. The story goes that when Omar conquered Jerusalem in the year 637, he asked the Christian Patriarch to show him the site of the Temple. For centuries the place had been used as a garbage dump and, at first, the Patriarch hesitated. In the end, he brought the Caliph there and Omar ordered the place cleared and had a wooden mosque erected.

The present, exquisite building was erected by Omar's successor, Abd el- Malik, and completed in 691. It stands over the living rock which Jews call 'the Foundation Stone' meaning that here the creation of the world was begun. Traditionally, this is where Abraham came to sacrifice Isaac. Here, David placed the Ark of the Covenant and Solomon made the Holy of Holies of the Temple. From this rock, in a vision, Mohammed sprang up to heaven and the dent made by his horse's phantom hoof is still indicated in the surface of the rock.

Octagonal in shape, the outside of the mosque is covered with beautiful marble panels, surmounted by blue and white Persian tiles. Within, the Dome is a glorious blaze of stucco and mosaic, with verses from the Koran inscribed in a golden frieze around the base of the dome. The sacred rock is enclosed within a carved wooden balustrade, while a flight of steps leads down into a cave in the rock known to the Moslems as 'the Well of Souls' where the dead are supposed to meet twice a week for prayer.

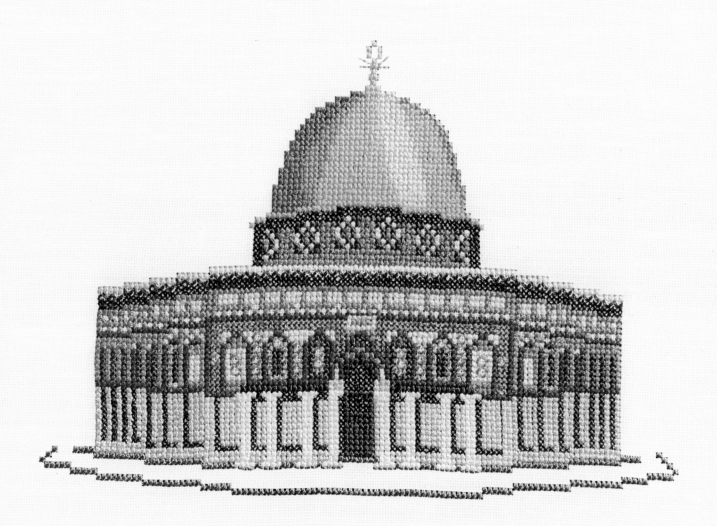

מנזר המצלבה

THE MONASTERY OF THE CROSS

At the foot of the hill where the Israel Museum is built, a beautiful valley lies, long a favorite promenade for Jerusalemites. In its midst, the strong and forbidding walls of the Monastery of the Cross remind one of the days when a church building had to be a fortress as well. This monastery is one of the oldest buildings in western Jerusalem.

There is an old legend that Lot came to this spot, fleeing from the destruction of Sodom, 'and dwelt in the hills... in a cave with his two daughters.' (Gen. 19:30) Here he planted saplings which grew into tall cypress trees, one of which is still shown to visitors in the courtyard of the monastery. In the days of Pontius Pilatus, the cross for Jesus' crucifixion was fashioned from one of these trees.

When Queen Helena, Emperor Constantine's mother, visited the Holy Land in the fourth century, she ordered a church and monastery built on the spot where the tree had grown. It was acquired by the Georgian (Russian) Orthodox Church in the seventh century, but since the 17th cent. it belongs to the Greek Orthodox Church.

Like most of the monuments in Jerusalem, it was destroyed and rebuilt and destroyed again. The present-day church was built in the 11th cent. and embellished by the Crusaders in the twelfth. The lovely silver cupola is a Crusader addition. Beautiful frescoes and a mosaic floor dating from the 16th cent. adorn its interior.

From the roof-top terrace of the monastery we have a beautiful view of the southern part of Jerusalem.

Today the Greek Government has undertaken extensive restoration work at the monastery which will be converted into a theological seminary.

שער שכם

DAMASCUS GATE

The walls that today encircle the Old City of Jerusalem were built by Sultan Suleiman the Magnificent (1520–1566) and were completed in 1538.

Eight gates in these walls connected the city with the outside world. Some were built over roads to other cities and were named for those cities. Thus, as the road to Damascus began from the central of the three gates in the northern wall, this was – and still is – known as the Damascus Gate. In Hebrew, since roads from Jerusalem no longer run so far, it is known as the 'Shechem Gate.'

The gateway was built on foundations that date from the city Hadrian built and named Aelia Capitolina in the vain hope of blotting Jerusalem off the world map forever, or perhaps even earlier. Indeed, Arabs still call it 'the Gate of the Column' in honor of the Roman column that stood there when they conquered the city in 637.

Set between two towers and topped by a wall crowned with battlements, the Damascus Gate is a fine example of Turkish architecture at its best and is the most beautiful of all the gates of Jerusalem.

Before 1898, when the wall by the Jaffa Gate was breached to allow the German Emperor Wilhelm II to ride in the Old City on horseback, the Damascus Gate was the ceremonial entrance to the Old City for many illustrious pilgrims.

Today the Damascus Gate is a very busy place, crowded with pilgrims, shoppers, tourists and peddlers. It forms the main link between the Arab quarter of the Old City and the new area of East Jerusalem outside the walls.

Near the Damascus Gate is the entrance to a famous cave called 'the Cave of Zedekiah' because it was through here that Zedekiah, the last king of Judah (597–586 B.C.E.), is said to have escaped from the beleaguered city at the time of the Babylonian siege.

pattern pa

יד אבשלום

THE PILLAR OF ABSALOM

The Bible recounts that Absalom, King David's rebellious son, who was childless, provided in his lifetime a burial-place and a funeral monument for himself: 'Now Absalom in his lifetime had taken and reared up for himself the pillar, which is in the King's dale, for he said: I have no son to keep my name in remembrance, and he called the pillar after his own name, and it is called Absalom's monument until this day.' (II Samuel 18, 18)

Although Absalom was killed in 'the forest of Ephraim,' in Transjordan, and cast into a pit in the forest, over which 'a very great heap of stones' was raised, an old and persistent tradition identifies the most beautiful among the funeral monuments in the Kidron valley, at the foot of the Mount of Olives, with the tomb of the rash and unfortunate prince.

In reality, the monument called 'the Pillar of Absalom' dates from a much later time. Its style is Hellenistic. Some authorities believe that it dates from the first century B.C.E., while others incline to the opinion that it was erected in the first century C.E., some time prior to the conquest of Jerusalem by the Romans.

The lower, quadrangular part of the monument was hewn out of the living rock. It is decorated with Ionian columns and contains a burial chamber. The upper part, a conus set on a round drum, is built of hewn stones. The total height of the Pillar of Absalom is twenty meters.

In old time, Arabs used to throw stones at the monument of the disobedient son, while Jews used to bring intractable children to this place, to punish them in front of the pillar illustrating the fruit of disobedience.

THE KENNEDY MEMORIAL

As a tribute to the memory of John F. Kennedy, President of the United States of America assassinated in 1963, who exemplified to many, in his short life, mankind's hope for universal peace and justice in our time, the Kennedy Memorial has been erected at the entrance of the John F. Kennedy Peace Forest.

The Memorial stands near the village of Aminadav, some five miles to the west of Ein Karem, not far from Jerusalem, on the highest peak in the area, 840 meters above sea-level, and is visible for miles around. The design for the monument was made by the Israeli architect David Reznik.

Seen from afar, the Memorial resembles the trunk of a giant tree, wantonly cut down before its time. The round structure is made up of fifty-one concrete pillars, representing the fifty States of the United States of America, plus the District of Columbia. Its height is 7.2 meters and its circumference 70 meters.

The interior of the Memorial is illuminated by an opening in the ceiling and by fifty high glass windows, each of them bearing the emblem of one of the fifty States.

Within the round hall, there is a relief-bust of John F. Kennedy and, in the middle, an 'eternal light,' which is a replica of the one burning on the tomb of the murdered President.

The man who declared: 'Prophecy is a Jewish tradition and Zionism the continuation of this long tradition,' is thus worthily commemorated in the Judaean Hills, the cradle of Israeli prophecy.

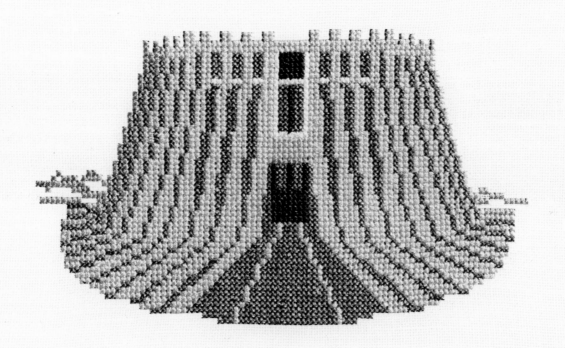

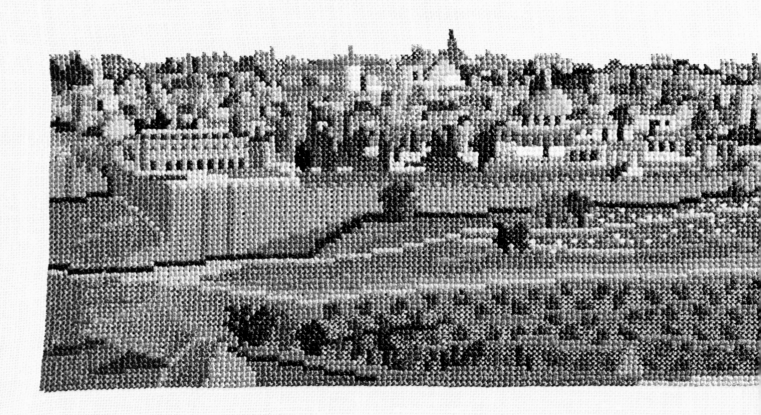

pattern page 56-57

בית הכנסת של האוניברסיטה העברית

THE HEBREW UNIVERSITY SYNAGOGUE

On the southern edge of the Hebrew University Campus in Jerusalem, in the area of the student dormitories, stands the 'Israel Goldstein Synagogue.'

This synagogue was built by means of generous gifts from members and friends of the B'nai Yeshurun Congregation in New York, in honor of their Rabbi, Dr. Israel Goldstein, on the occasion of his 60th birthday. Designed and built by the Israeli architects Heinz Rau and David Reznik, the synagogue was dedicated in August 1957.

Considerable interest has been aroused by the unusual design of this building, which embodied a new approach to modern synagogue architecture. The synagogue is built on a platform supported by eight pillars forming wide arches, and is covered by a big elliptical dome.

The area beneath the platform has been laid out as a garden, at the end of which a staircase leads up to the synagogue.

Light enters the synagogue through windows ranged peripherally at floor level and flows upward following the lines of the cupola, thus creating a singularly striking effect. The subdued and peaceful atmosphere thus created is an inducement to meditation.
Besides regular religious services, weddings of students, members of the University's staff and their families are celebrated in this beautiful synagogue.

The brilliant white dome of the University Synagogue has become one of the familiar landmarks of modern Jerusalem.

pattern page

כנסיית ההלקאה

THE CHAPEL OF THE FLAGELLATION

A tradition dating from the Middle Ages places the Praetorium in which the Roman procurator Pontius Pilatus judged and sentenced Jesus in the Antonia fortress in the north-western corner of the Temple platform.

The Antonia was destroyed by Titus, when he conquered Jerusalem. On part of the site, the Turks built a barracks which later served as an Arab boys' school. This is now 'the First Station' of the Way of the Cross.

Another part of the site of Antonia is occupied at present by the Convent of the Sisters of Zion, where a portion of the Roman pavement, the Lithostrotos mentioned by St. John, has been uncovered.

It was a Roman custom to flagellate the condemned prior to their crucifixion. Jesus did not escape this cruel treatment. Indeed, the Gospel of St. John (19, 1) says: 'Then Pilate therefore took Jesus and scourged him.'

A small church was built by the friars of the Franciscan order on the place where, according to tradition, the flagellation of Jesus took place, within the precincts of the Antonia fortress.

This is the Chapel of the Flagellation, a building of exquisite taste, decorated with beautiful stained-glass windows.

It is part of the Franciscan Monastery of the Flagellation which houses the Biblical Institute of the Order and an interesting archaeological museum.

כנסיית הקבר

THE CHURCH OF THE HOLY SEPULCHRE

Holiest of all Holy Places to Christians all over the world, the Church of the Holy Sepulchre was built over the traditional sites of Golgotha and the tomb of Jesus. All through the generations, this has been the goal of innumerable pilgrims, who faced undaunted the perils of the journey by land and sea. For this holy place the Crusades were fought.

Today, prelates and pilgrims come to these holy places from every corner of the globe, filling the ancient chapels and corridors with the sounds of strange liturgies and whispered prayers and comments in every language.

The present, largely Crusader church, completed in 1149, stands on the site of the great basilica built by the Emperor Constantine over the places identified by his mother, the saintly Queen Helena, as the Hill of Golgotha (Calvary) and the burial place of Jesus.

The main part of the church is the rotunda under the big cupola, in the center of which stands the marble aedicule of the Holy Sepulchre.

When Saladin defeated the Crusaders (1187), he gave the care of the shrine into Moslem hands, and they remain its official guardians. Over the years, rights within the church were apportioned among the different Christian communities, who have their own chapels within the church. All the Christian sects — Roman Catholic, Greek, Armenian, Copt, Syrian and Abyssinian — serve the shrine, celebrating the great Christian festivals according to their different calendars, in a sequence of sumptuous rituals, rich vestments and glorious music.

דרך היסורים

VIA DOLOROSA

'The Painful Way,' which in Latin is Via Dolorosa, is the name given to the route of Jesus' last journey from the Praetorium, where He was judged, scourged and sentenced to death, to Golgotha, the place of His crucifixion. Every Friday, pious Christians retrace 'the Way of the Cross' through the narrow alleys of Old Jerusalem to the traditional site of Golgotha in the Church of the Holy Sepulchre. On Good Friday, the path is followed with particular solemnity.

The Way of the Cross is divided into fourteen stations, each commemorating an episode of Jesus' progress on the first Good Friday. Some of the incidents are recorded in the Gospels, some based on legend.

From the first station in the Praetorium, identified as the ancient fortress of the Antonia, the second one is at the spot where Jesus was forced to shoulder the cross. At the third, near the ancient Roman arch known as 'Ecce Homo' ('Behold the man'), He fell for the first time. At the fourth, He saw His mother fainting and, at the fifth, the Roman soldiers grabbed a bystander, Simon the Cyrenian, and obliged him to help carry the cross. At the sixth station, the pious Veronica wiped Jesus' sweating face and received a true image ('vera icone') on her veil. The veil, still bearing the imprint of the holy features, is preserved in St. Peter's at Rome. The seventh station marks the spot where Jesus fell for the second time. At the eighth, He addressed 'the daughters of Jerusalem' who wept for Him (Luke 23:28–31) and the ninth marks the spot where He fell for the third time.

The last five stations are within the Church of the Holy Sepulchre. They mark the places where Jesus was stripped of His garments; where He was nailed to the cross and where He died; where His body was delivered to His mother; and, finally, the place where He was buried, which is called by the Greeks 'Anastasis', the Resurrection.

pattern page

מגדל דוד

THE CITADEL – TOWER OF DAVID

Popular tradition has attached the name of David to this site from early times. It was known as 'the Tower of David' even before the conquest of Jerusalem by the Arabs.

In fact, there is no historical connection between David and the site of the citadel. It was Herod, a great and enthusiastic builder, who built himself a fortified palace here towards the end of the 1st century B.C.E. Josephus, who saw the palace before its destruction, describes it admiringly: 'He built himself a palace in the Upper City, raising the rooms to a very great height and adorning them with the most costly furniture of gold and marble seats and beds; and they were so large that they could contain very many companies of men.'

The palace was protected by a complex of three mighty towers which the king named 'Mariamne' in memory of his Hasmonean wife, 'Phasael' in honor of his brother, and 'Hippicus' after one of his friends.

Titus left them all standing after 70 C.E., to show what the Romans had been up against in their defeat of the Jews. When Hadrian again razed Jerusalem in 135 and rebuilt it as the Roman city of Aelia Capitolina, he, too, left part of the Phasael Tower standing. The massive stonework at its base marks it clearly as Herodian.

However, the imposing ramparts to be seen today are mainly Turkish, on Crusader foundations. This tower, with its graceful minaret, is entirely Turkish, built by Suleiman the Magnificent in the 16th century, the minaret being added in 1655. In Arabic, it is called 'el Qalaa', the Citadel, but to Jews and Christians, it remains 'the Tower of David.'

בסיית כל האומות

THE CHURCH OF ALL NATIONS

After the Last Supper, Jesus went out with his disciples to the grove of Gethsemane, at the foot of the Mount of Olives. There he 'withdrew from them about a stone's cast, kneeled down and prayed ... and being in an agony, he prayed more earnestly and his sweat was as it were great drops of blood falling down on the ground.' (Luke 22, 41–44)

On this place, called the Rock of Agony, a Byzantine church was erected towards the end of the fourth century, only to be destroyed, together with other shrines, in the Persian invasion of 614.

The Crusaders built another church on the site in the twelfth century and entrusted it to the Benedictine Order.

The present church, built on the site of the ancient basilica, was designed for the Franciscan order, which now owns Gethsemane, by the Italian architect A. Barluzzi. The foundation-stone was laid in 1919 by the Cardinal Giustini and the construction was completed in 1925.

The cost of building was met by contributions from Catholic communities all over the world, and the coats-of-arms of the contributing nations form an important part of the interior decoration. Hence the name 'Church of All Nations.'

Part of the rock, mosaics of the ancient pavement and other features of the Byzantine church have been left visible.

The church is notable for its roof with twelve cupolas, its columned and gabled façade and the magnificent mosaic on the gable, showing Jesus kneeling in prayer on the Rock of Agony.

הכנסיה הרוסית

THE RUSSIAN CATHEDRAL

This beautiful cathedral, with its striking green domes, dominates the Russian Compound, a large enclosed area in west Jerusalem, built in the years following the Crimean War, when it also included a monastery, hospice and hospital.

In the ninteenth century, Russia, which always considered herself the heiress of the Byzantine empire, assumed the protectorship of the Orthodox Church in the Ottoman Empire and, particularly, in the Holy Land, then part of it. So important was this role in the eyes of Czarist Russia that, to impose its recognition by the unwilling Sultan, she did not hesitate to declare war on Turkey in 1853. Despite her defeat, Russia continued to manifest an even increased interest in the welfare of the church in Jerusalem. The Russian Compound was built to provide accommodation and spiritual and medical care for the many thousands of Russian pilgrims that used to visit the holy places every year before the First World War.

In Mandate times, the British authorities occupied and used the buildings for administrative purposes. After the establishment of the state of Israel, the Israeli government bought the compound, with the exception of the cathedral which remains the property of the Russian Orthodox Church.

In ancient times, the area in front of the cathedral is known to have been a quarry. A cracked, partly fashioned stone column, 12 meters long, can still be seen lying there. Its dimensions fit Josephus' description of the colonnade of Herod's Temple. Quite probably, the column cracked while it was being fashioned to take its place in the Temple, and was abandoned by the cutters still attached to the bedrock. People used to call the column 'a finger of the giant Og, king of Bashan.'

טחנת הרוח של מונטיפיורי

THE WINDMILL OF MONTEFIORE

The visitor to Jerusalem, who strolls along King David Street, suddenly reaches a small garden, in the middle of which stands a white windmill. A strange sight, when seen for the first time. A fragment of a Dutch landscape in the stern scene of modern Jerusalem, with the walls of the Old City and Mount Zion as a background. But standing there for over a hundred years, the windmill has become a familiar landmark, which nobody would want to miss in the panorama of Jerusalem.

Beautiful as it looks, the windmill was not built merely for the sake of beauty. In the mind of its builder, the great Jewish philanthropist Sir Moses Montefiore, its purpose was a practical one. The windmill was meant to actually grind corn and provide some employment for Jews who would be courageous enough to leave the security of the City walls and and settle in the new quarter of Yemin Moshe, founded in the year 1860, to start an existence based on productive work instead of relying on charitable donations from overseas.

It is only fair to add that the quarter of Yemin Moshe, founded by Sir Moses Montefiore, was largely built with funds left for this purpose by the American Jewish philanthropist Judah Touro. This is why the quarter was also called 'Batei Touro' (the Houses of Touro).

Despite the many difficulties which marked its beginnings, Yemin Moshe represents the first decisive step in the development of modern Jewish Jerusalem. Partly abandoned as insecure during the period when Jerusalem was partitioned, it is now being rebuilt and modernized, to become a residential quarter for artists and a center of artistic activity.

INSTRUCTIONS

The color illustrations in this book show the embroidery in its original size. The needlework is mainly cross-stich, or occasionally straight stitch, for which directions are given separately with each pattern.

For these designs, fine canvas with 14 threads per cm^2 was used. Color indications for each design are given according to the color-chart of D.M.C. embroidery silk. Each square in the design represents 2 threads of material and one cross stitch.

On this fine canvas, 2 strands of silk were used for 2 threads of material. Where only one strand was used, it is indicated beside the number with a [1], e.g., 3021 [1]. When using coarser linen, the thickness of the silk should be increased, in which case it is preferable to use 3 strands for 2 threads of material and 2 strands for the numbers indicated with [1].

Some designs, e.g., 'A View of Jerusalem,' the old mosaik, and the menorah, are very suitable for tapestry-work in wool (with half stitches on a very coarse canvas of about 4 squares per cm). However, it is not possible to indicate the appropriate shade numbers, as these vary with different brands of wool. If using wool, refer to the D.M.C. color-chart which is available in every needlework shop. This method calls for a background of a light or dark color. Suggested uses of these tapestries are: a tecosy of the menorah, a cushion of the old mosaic, or a big wall tapestry of 'A View of Jerusalem.'

To avoid confusing the shades, you may find it helpful to stick a thread of the appropriate color beside each number. In general, it is preferable to start with the darkest colors.

Practical suggestions for the embroidery are to be found on pages 43–45 of this booklet.

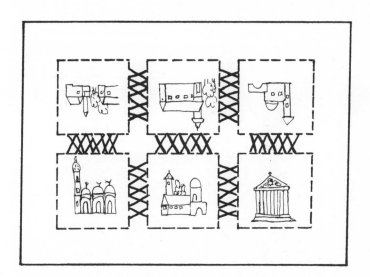

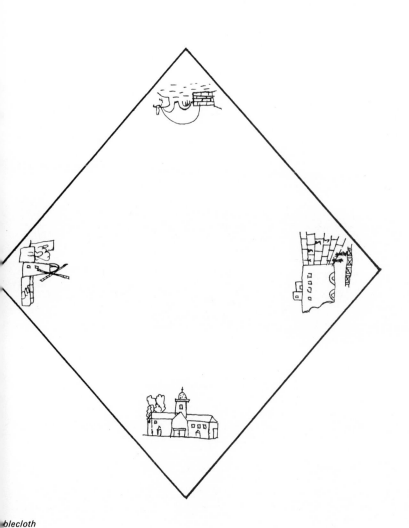

handbags

tablecloth

...blecloth

lampshade

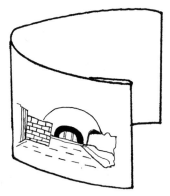

book cover

picture book

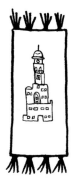

bookmark

greeting cards

tallith bag (praying shawl bag)

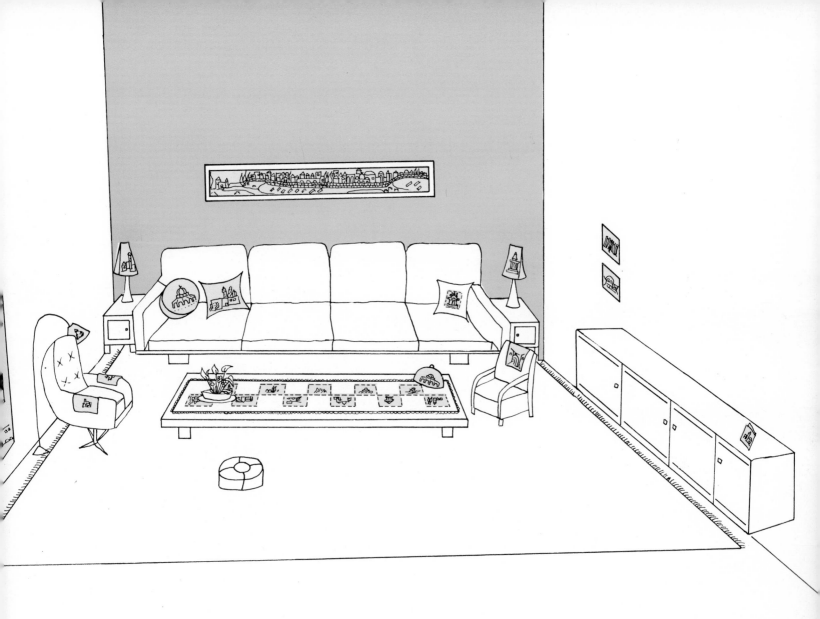

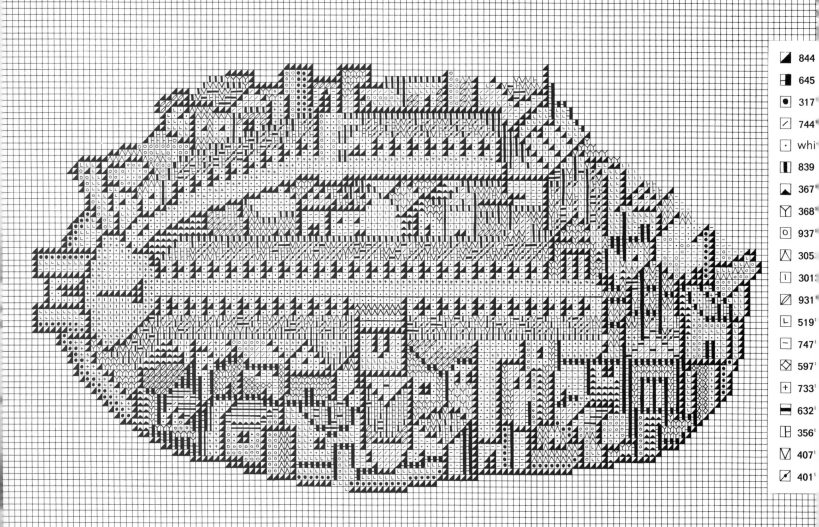

844
645
317
744
whi
839
367
368
937
305
301
931
519
747
597
733
632
356
407
401

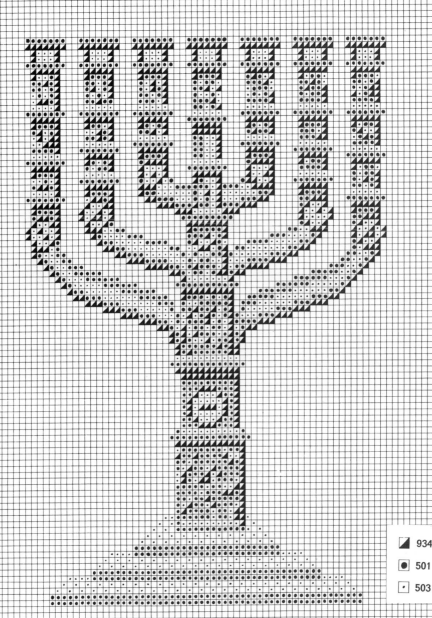

934

501

503

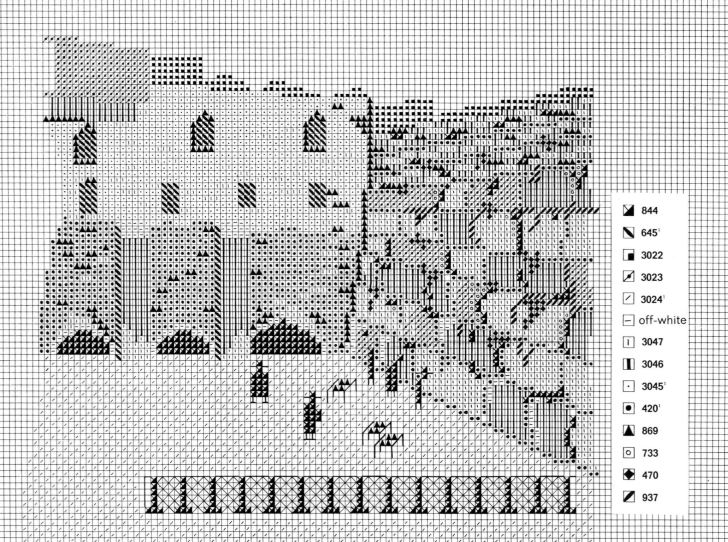

The fence in the foreground with 844, the table-legs with 869

◪	844
◩	645[1]
◪	3022
▨	3023
◿	3024[1]
−	off-white
		3047
▮	3046
·	3045[1]
●	420[1]
▲	869
○	733
◆	470
◪	937

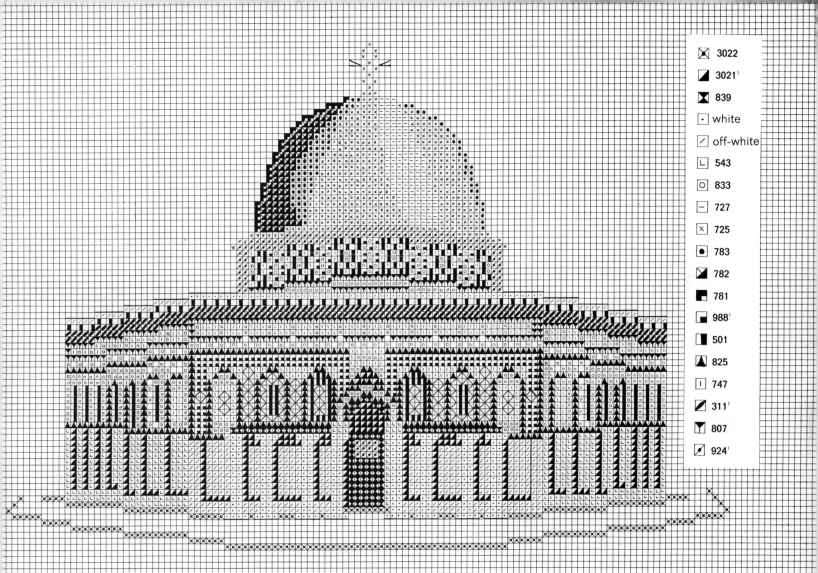

⊠	3022
◪	3021'
⊠	839
·	white
⁄	off-white
⌊	543
◯	833
−	727
⊠	725
●	783
◪	782
◪	781
◪	988'
◪	501
▲	825
I	747
◪	311'
�⊤	807
◪	924'

The windows with 833, the contours at the base of the building with 3022, the lines on both sides of the dome with 747, the window-line with 3021',
with 725 the lines on top of the dome

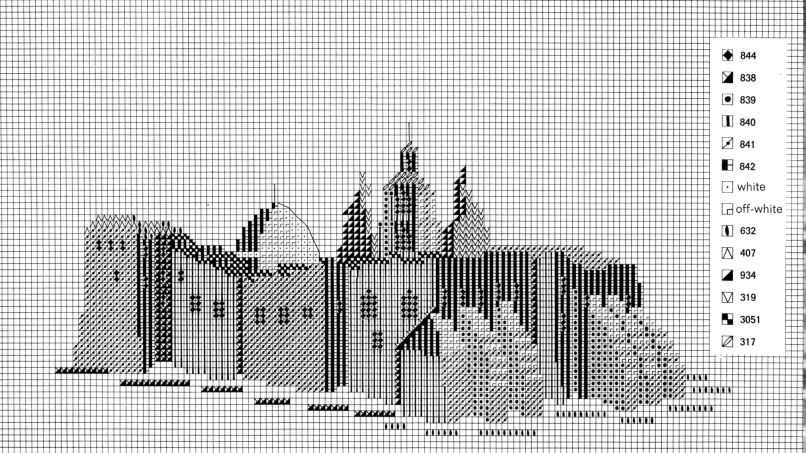

◆	844
◤	838
●	839
▯	840
◿	841
▣	842
·	white
⌐	off-white
◖	632
◿	407
◢	934
▽	319
▰	3051
⧄	317

Outline of the dome and the line on top with 842, the line of the tower in the middle with 317

■	844
▲	801
⊟	869
⊙	420
◪	3045
◫	3046
⊠	3047
·	422
◪	3021[1]
◫	3022
▯	3024
⊠	934
◫	937
└	470
◧	319
◆	355
⊡	839[1]
⊟	613[1]
◩	611

The lines of the battlements with 801

51

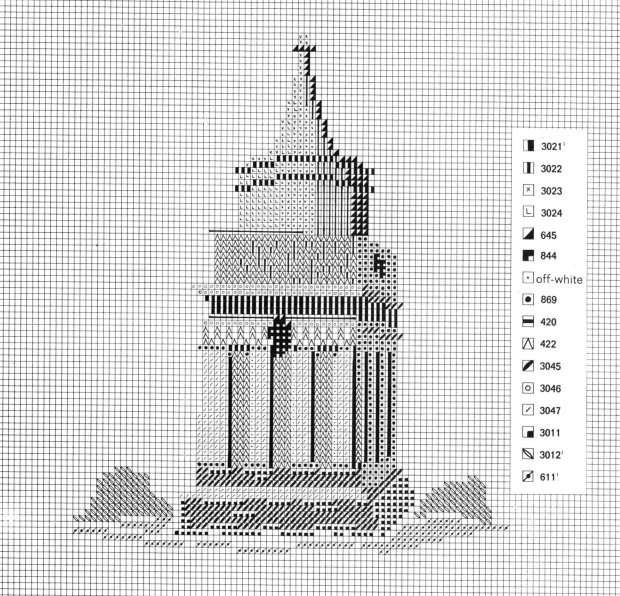

3021'
3022
3023
3024
645
844
off-white
869
420
422
3045
3046
3047
3011
3012'
611'

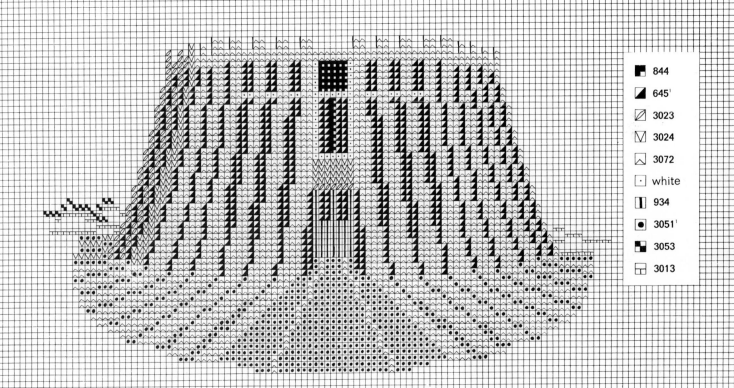

■	844
◪	645¹
▨	3023
⋁	3024
⌃	3072
·	white
❙	934
⬢	3051¹
▚	3053
⊞	3013

All lines with 645¹

53

■	844
◉	645¹
◪	3024
·	white
⊟	840
◆	841
⊠	3022
◢	319
⊠	3053¹
▯	3013¹
◪	368
▲	3045
◪	3046
⊻	937¹
⊟	927¹
⊙	367

Outline the dome with 927¹ and the windows and doors with 844

◨	838
◪	3021
◥	420
◧	3045
⊙	3046
⧄	3047
◣	833
⊙	3022
⋀	3023
·	3024
⊠	934
⊟	937
∟	470
▊	319
◆	367
⊻	3012
−	3013
Ⓢ	356
◨	926

The star on the roof with 3021

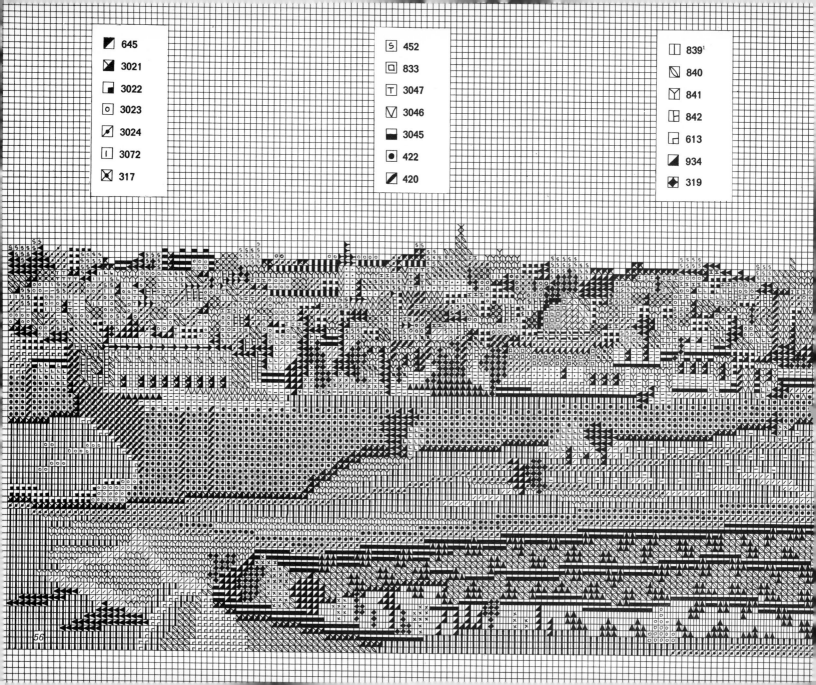

645
3021
3022
3023
3024
3072
317

452
833
3047
3046
3045
422
420

839
840
841
842
613
934
319

56

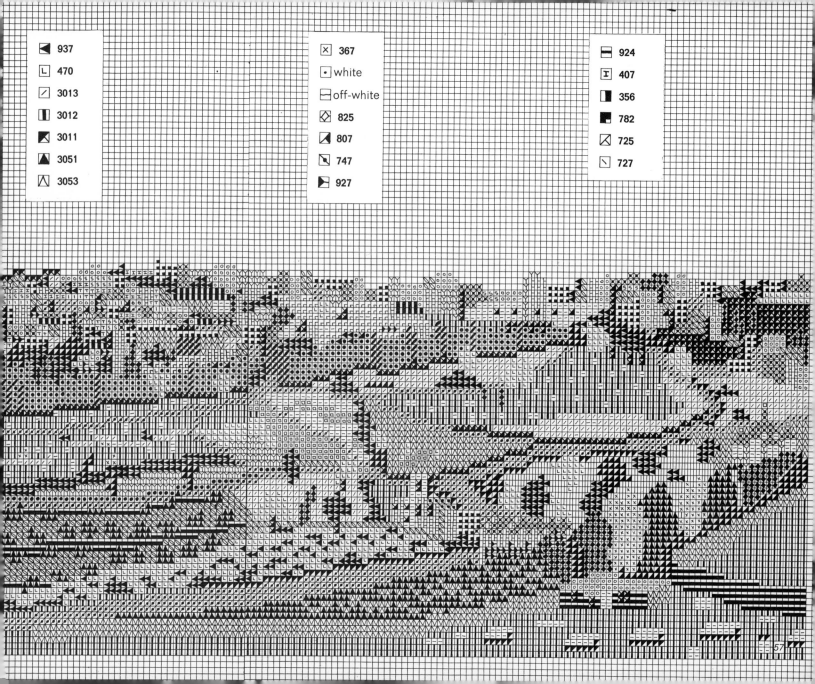

937
470
3013
3012
3011
3051
3053

367
white
off-white
825
807
747
927

924
407
356
782
725
727

■	844
▲	645
●	3022
✕	3023
⌐	3024
◿	3072
◥	3021[1]
▼	838[1]
▯	839[1]
△	840
◇	841
'	842
Y	407
·	white
−	off-white
◖	924
◿	926
◪	927
⊠	747
◪	613
○	612
◣	833

The lines in the upper-left windows with 613, the line on the dome and the parapet with 844, windows on the upper-right side with white straight stitches (see the picture)

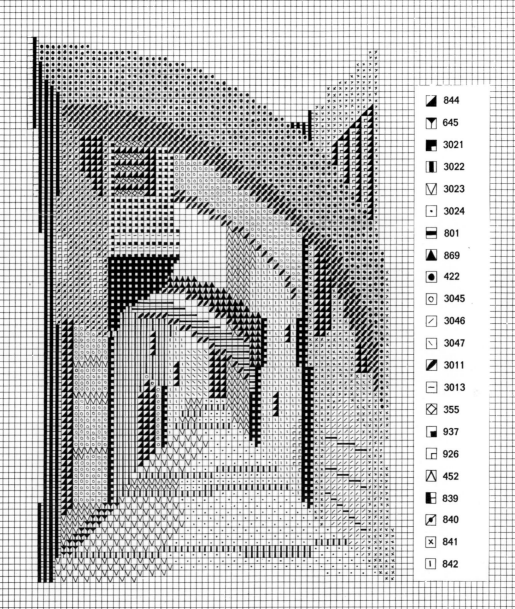

◤	844
▼	645
◧	3021
▯	3022
▽	3023
·	3024
▬	801
▲	869
●	422
○	3045
╱	3046
╲	3047
◪	3011
▭	3013
◇	355
◧	937
⊓	926
△	452
▤	839
◪	840
⊠	841
⊔	842

	844
	3022
	801
	869
	420
	3045
	422
	3047
	782
	612
	611
	934
	937
	470
	319
	3013
	3011
	613

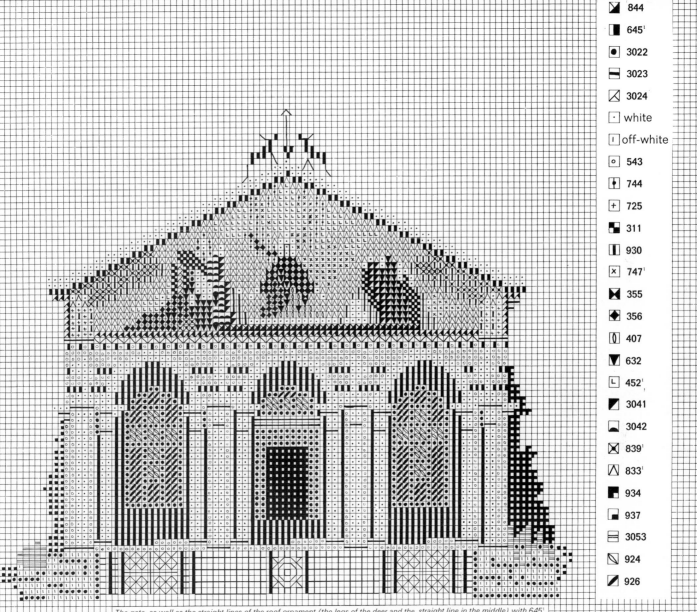

◪	844
◨	645¹
⊙	3022
⊟	3023
◩	3024
·	white
I	off-white
⊙	543
⯭	744
+	725
◪	311
⊞	930
✕	747¹
◪	355
◆	356
◖◗	407
▼	632
L	452¹
◹	3041
◠	3042
⊠	839¹
◺	833¹
◼	934
◻	937
⊟	3053
◩	924
◪	926

The gate, as well as the straight lines of the roof ornament (the legs of the deer and the straight line in the middle) with 645¹,
the straight stitches over the white arches with 3022

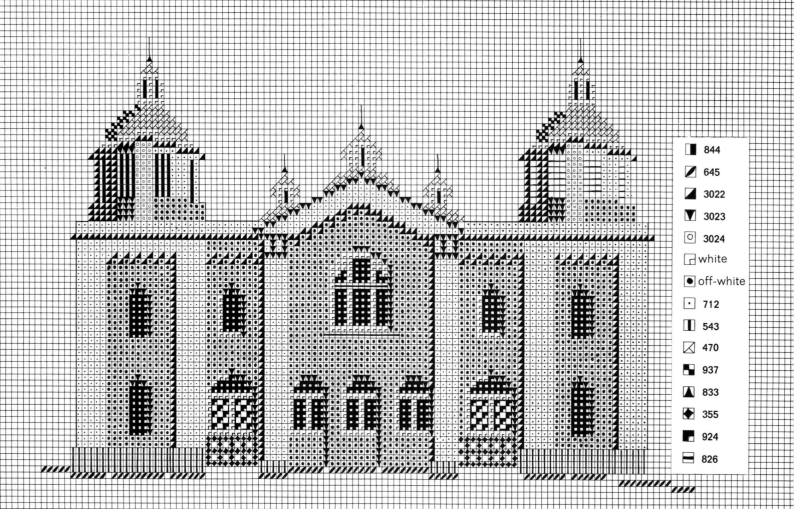

	844
	645
	3022
	3023
⊙	3024
	white
●	off-white
·	712
	543
	470
	937
▲	833
◆	355
	924
	826

All the lines on the towers with 844, the left-side outline of the building with 645 and that of the right-hand side with 926.
The right-hand side of the two big towers and the top of the building also with 926. The doors with 924. The windows in the tower on the right with 645

✖	844
◪	3021
◩	869
◣	420
◮	3045
▬	422
⊙	3046
·	3047
∧	white
−	off-white
◳	839
◫	838
⬦	842¹
◈	934
⊟	319
◹	937
⊡	470
⁄	3013¹
⊻	501¹
◤	3501¹
⊞	3022
+	317¹

The vanes, the gate and the windows with 844

63

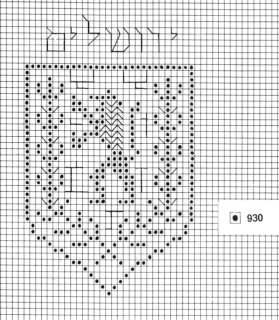

שושן פורים

● 930

All lines with 930